This Coloring Book Belongs to:

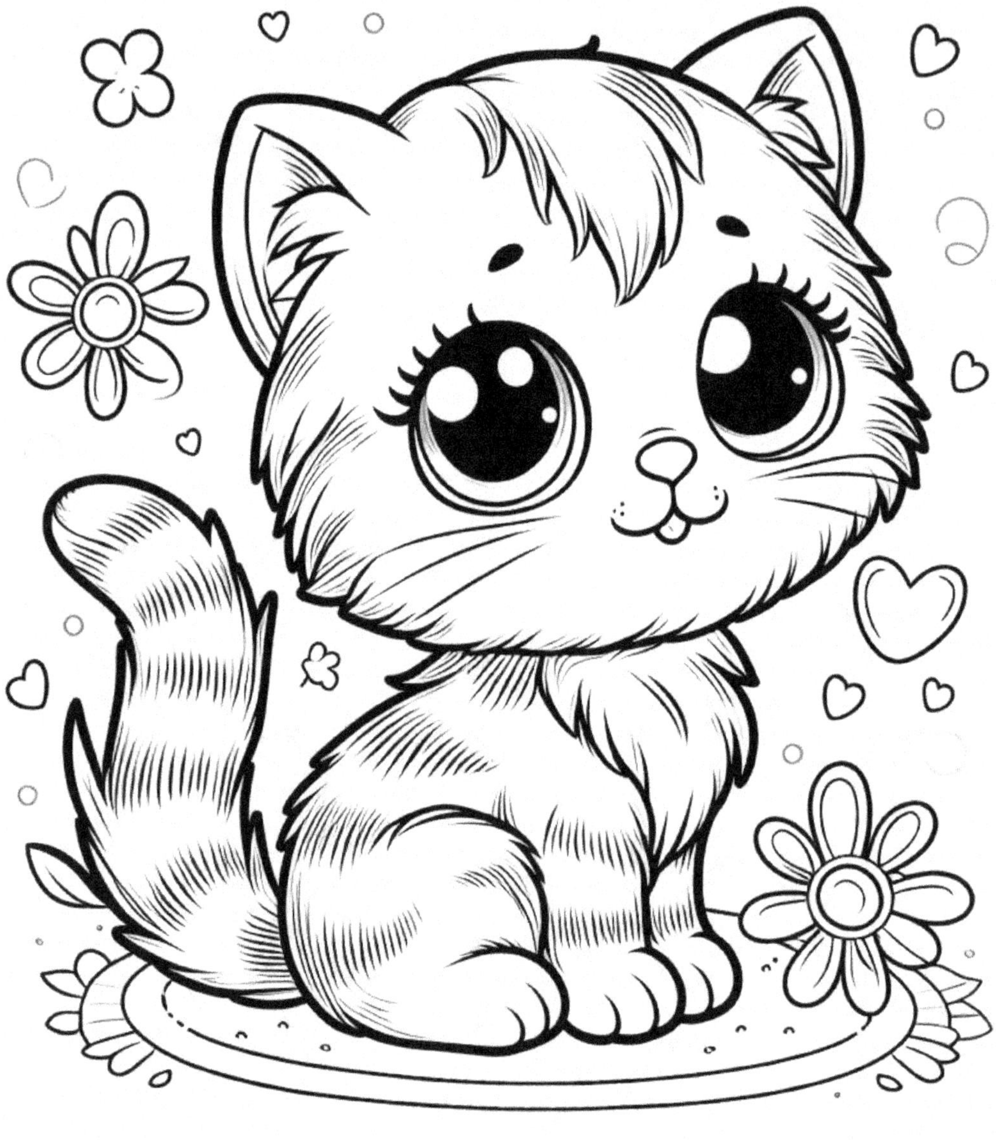

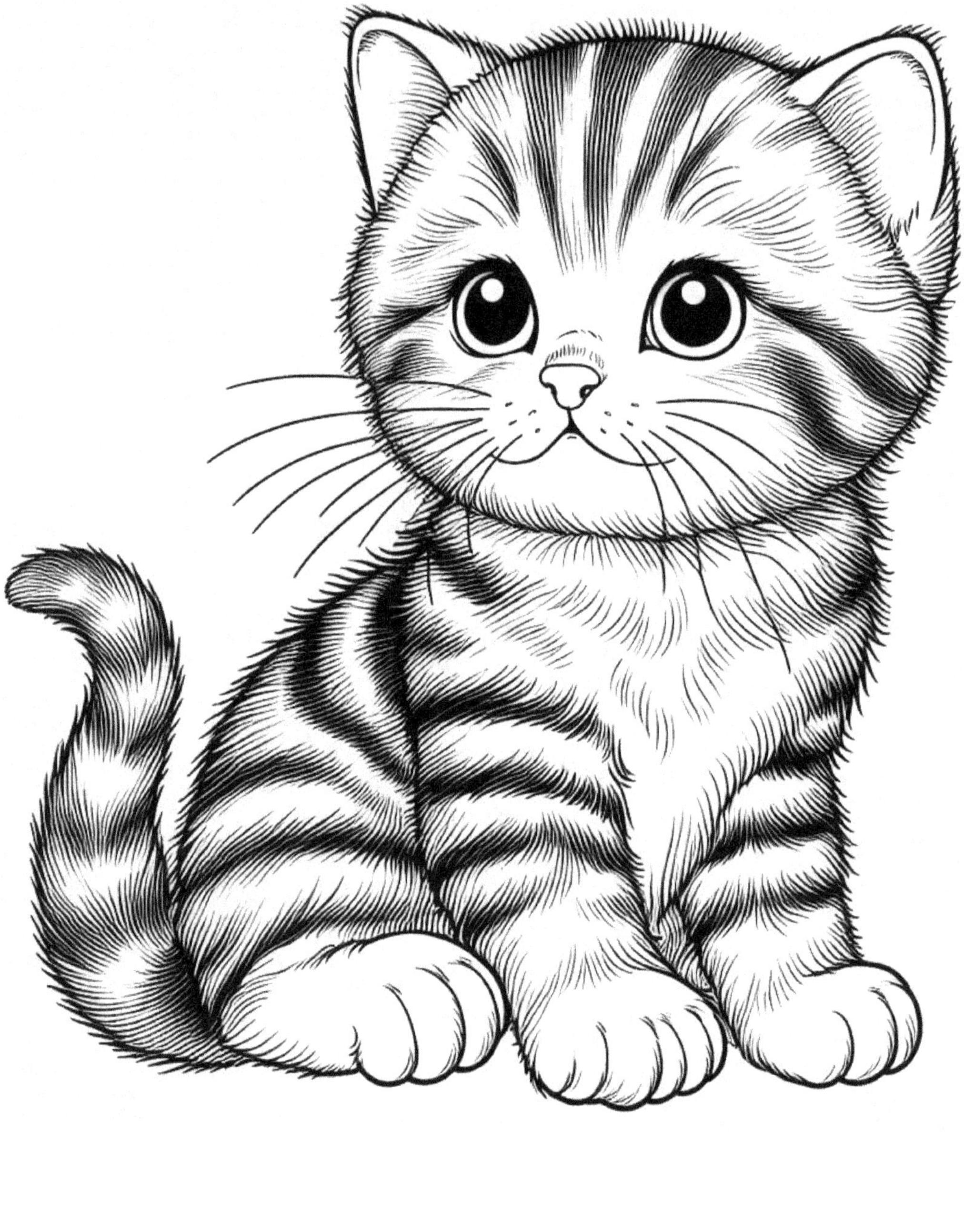

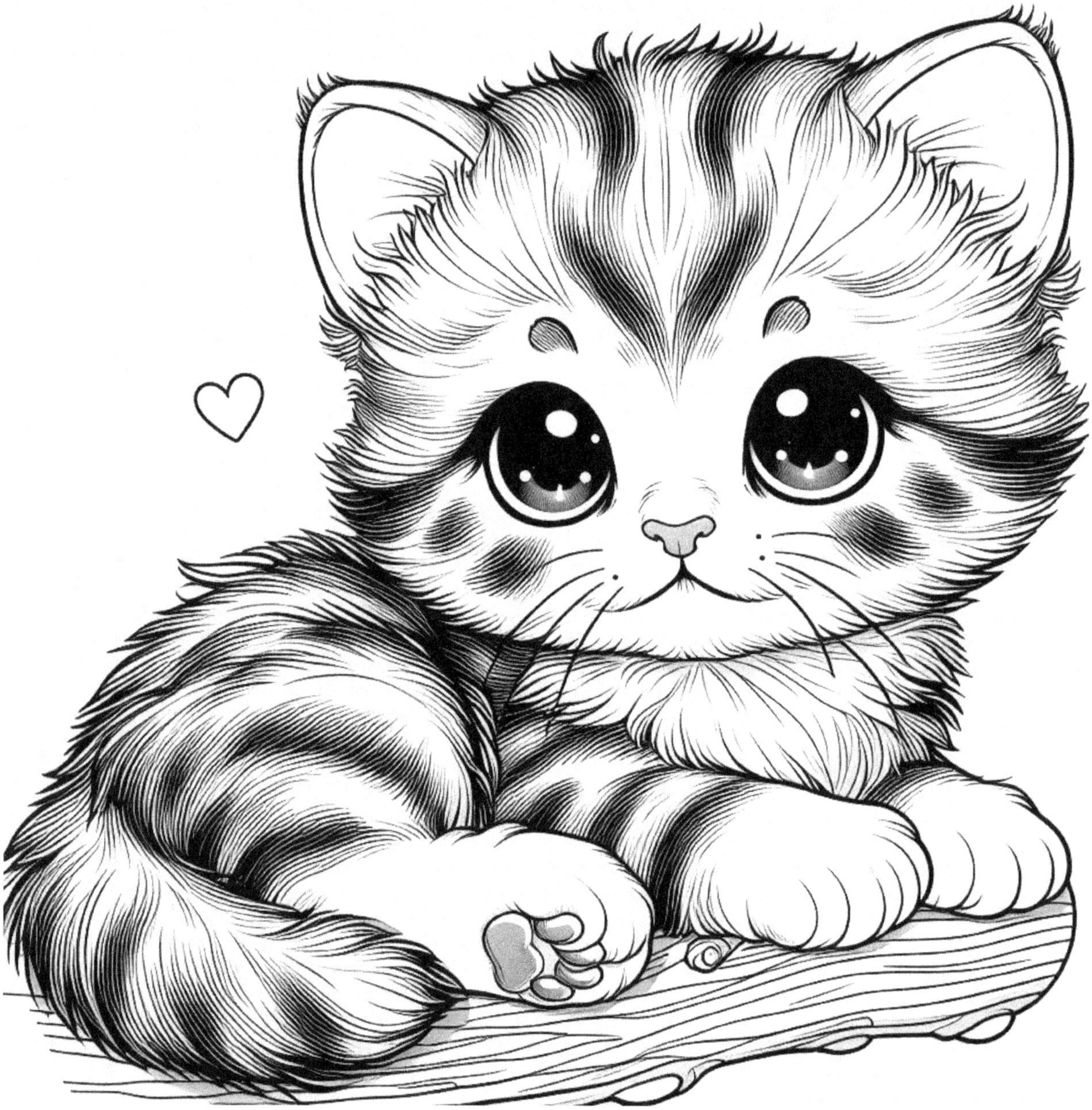

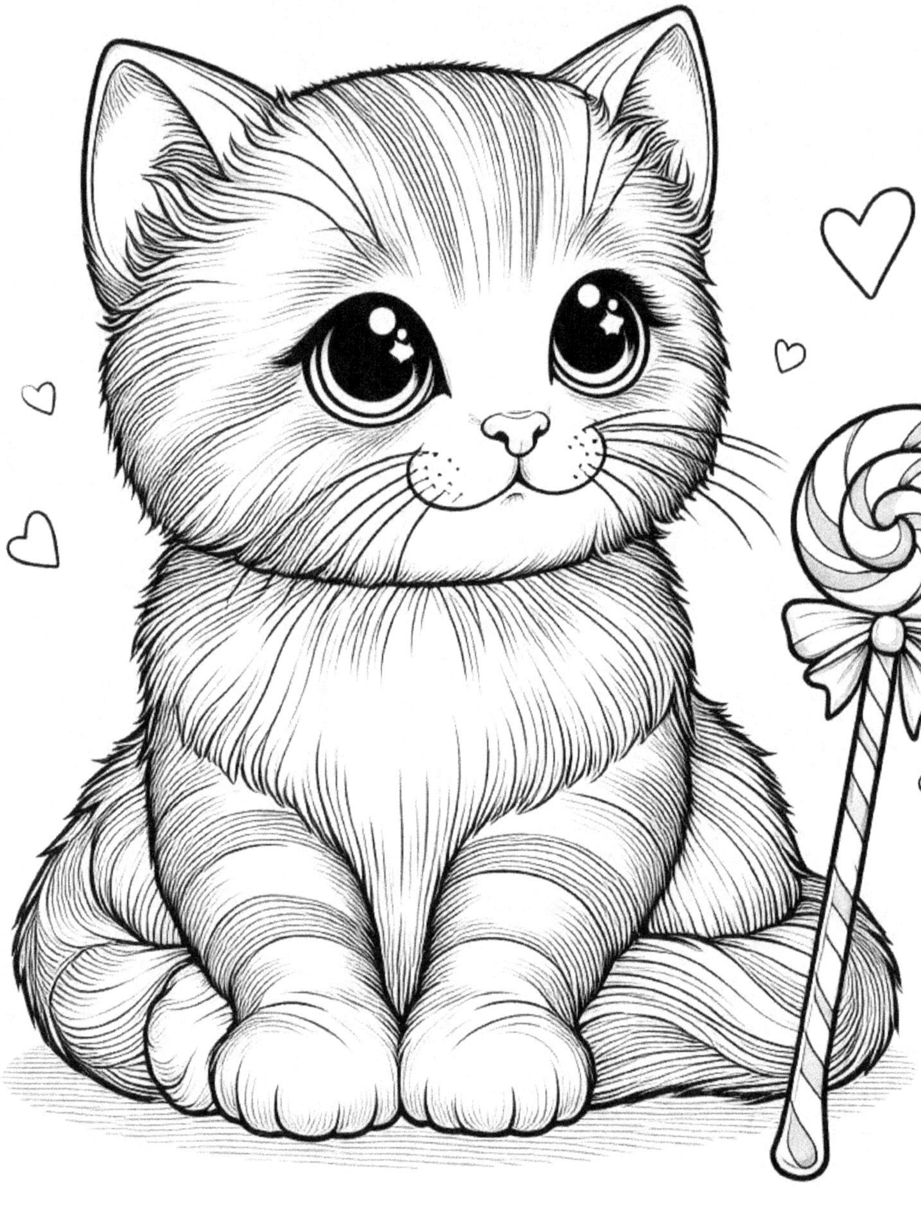

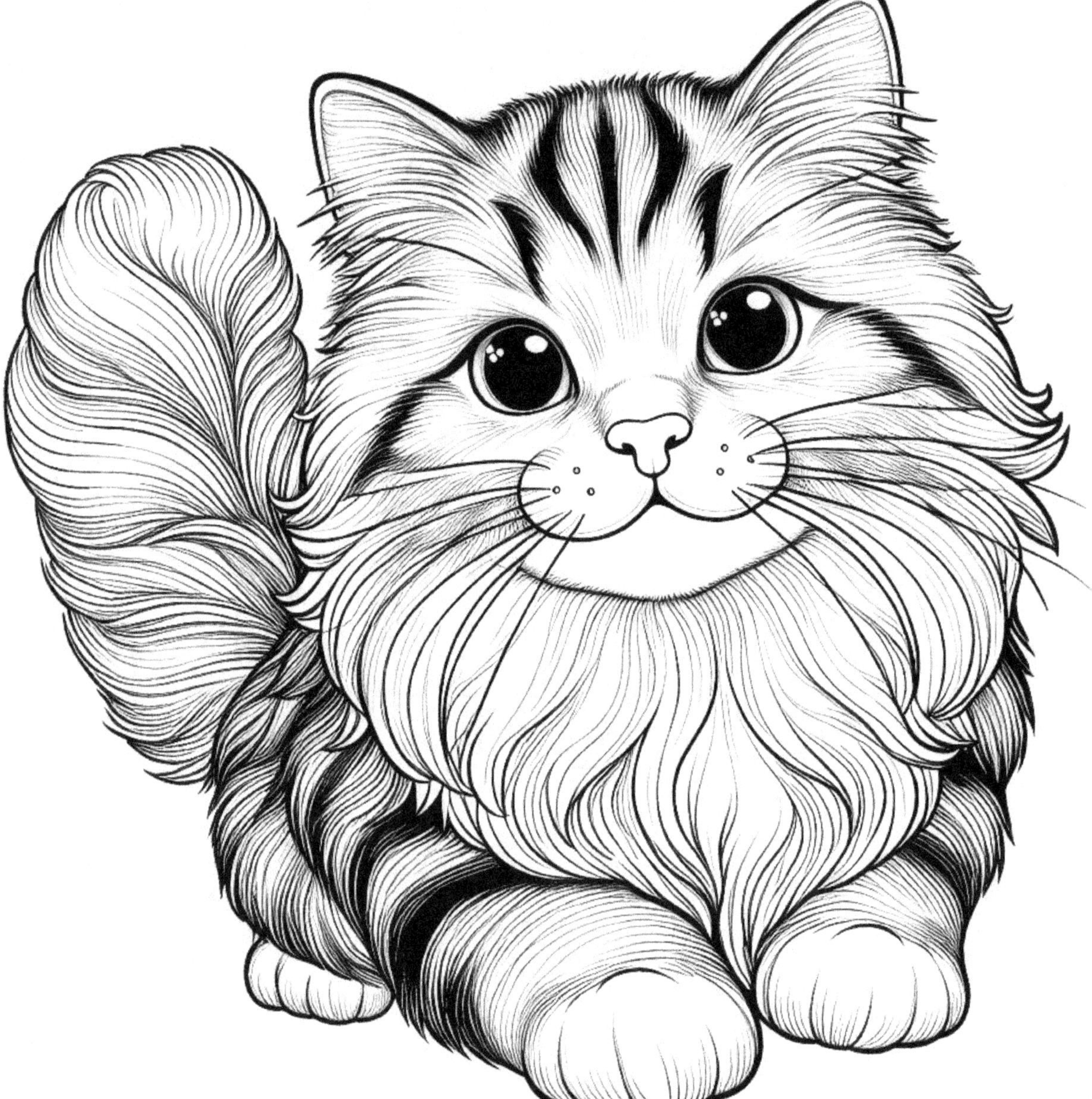

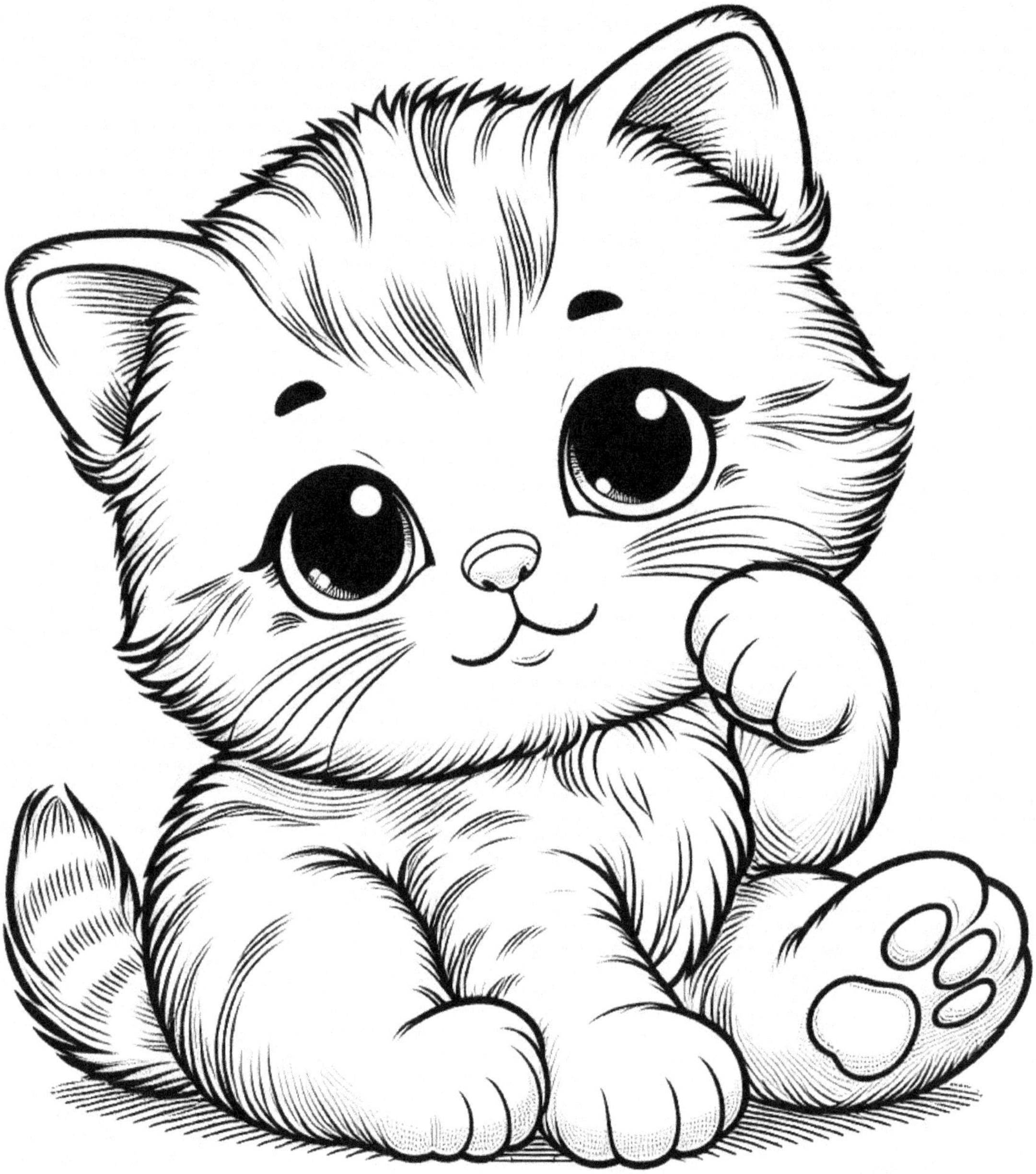

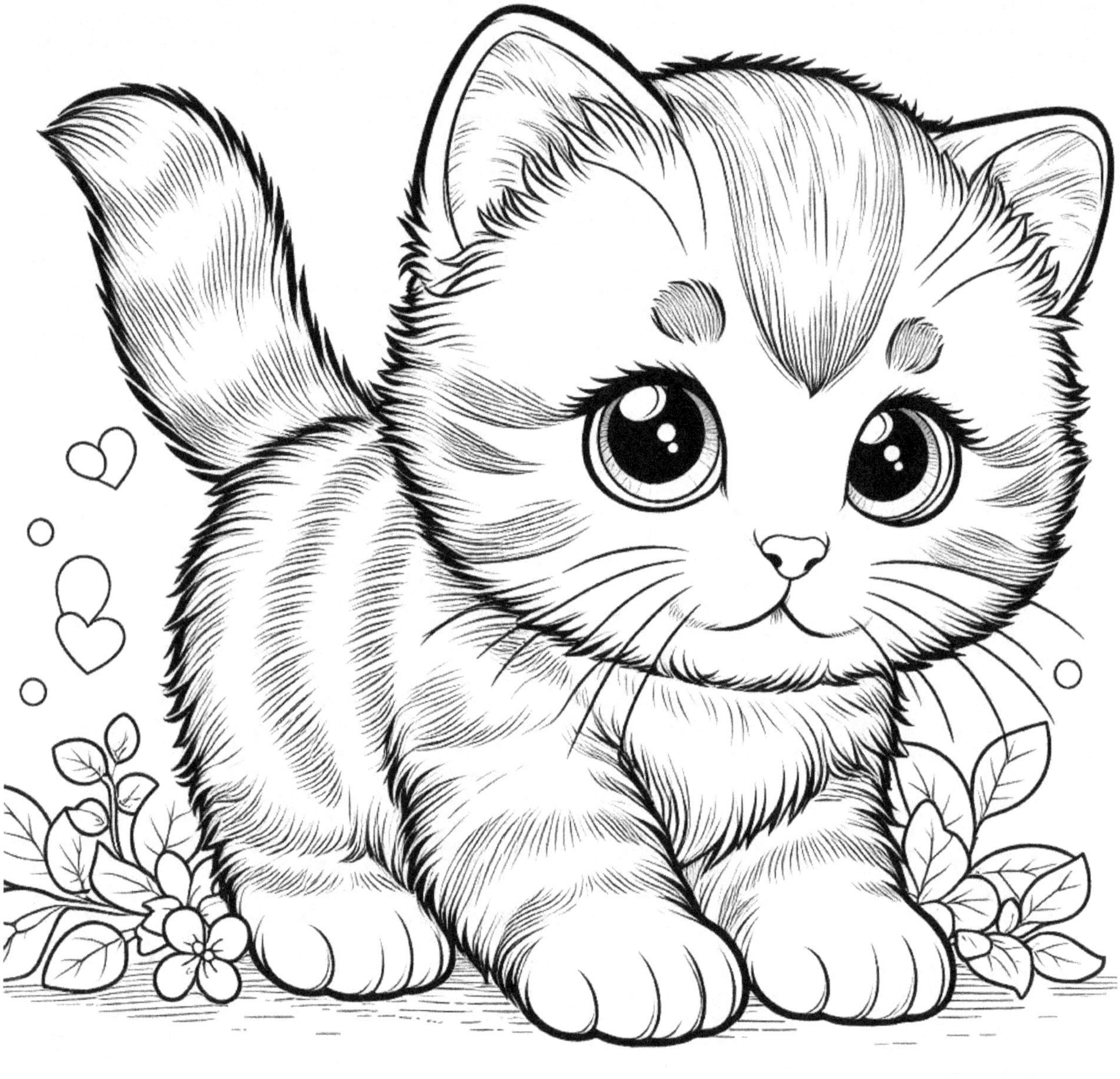

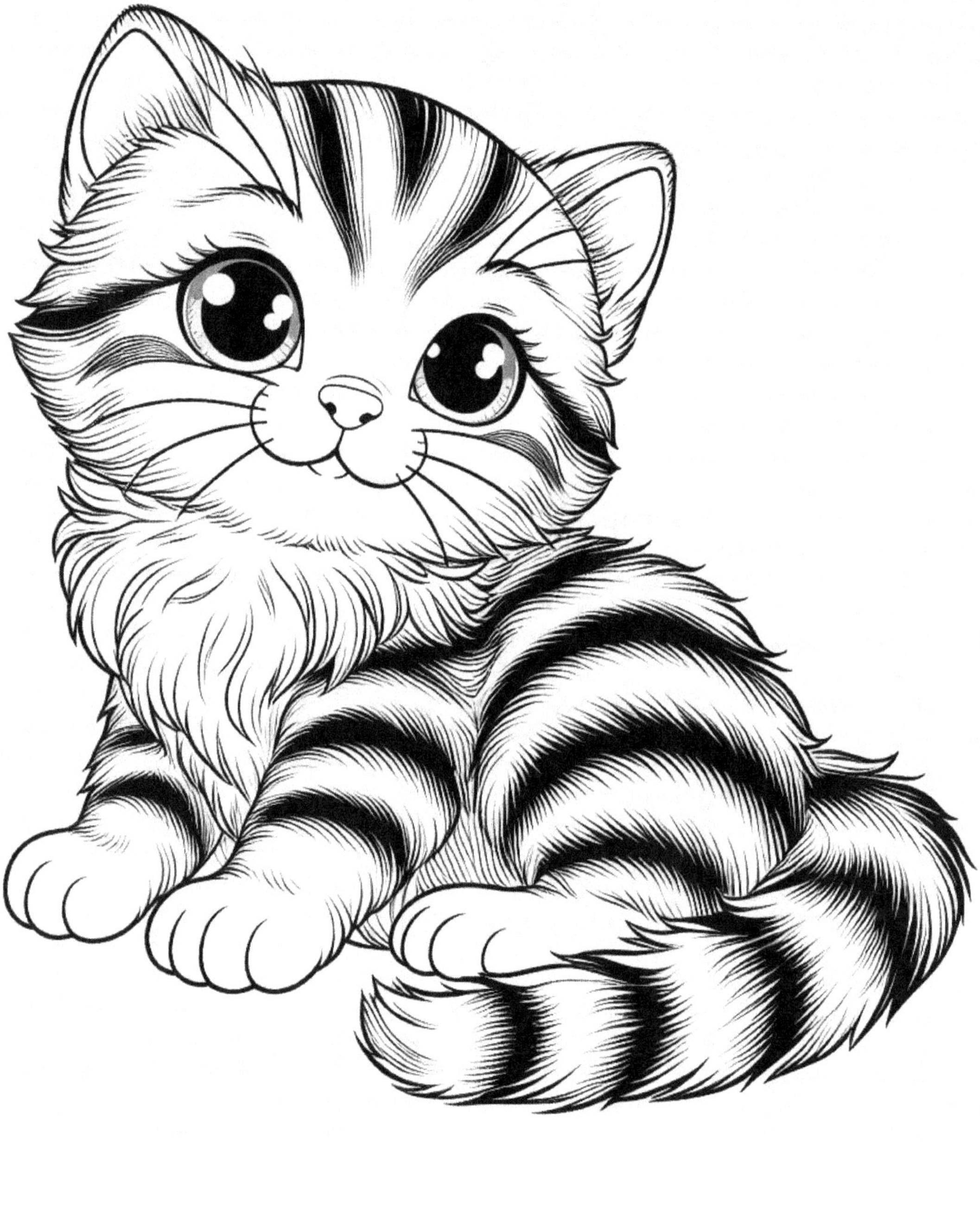

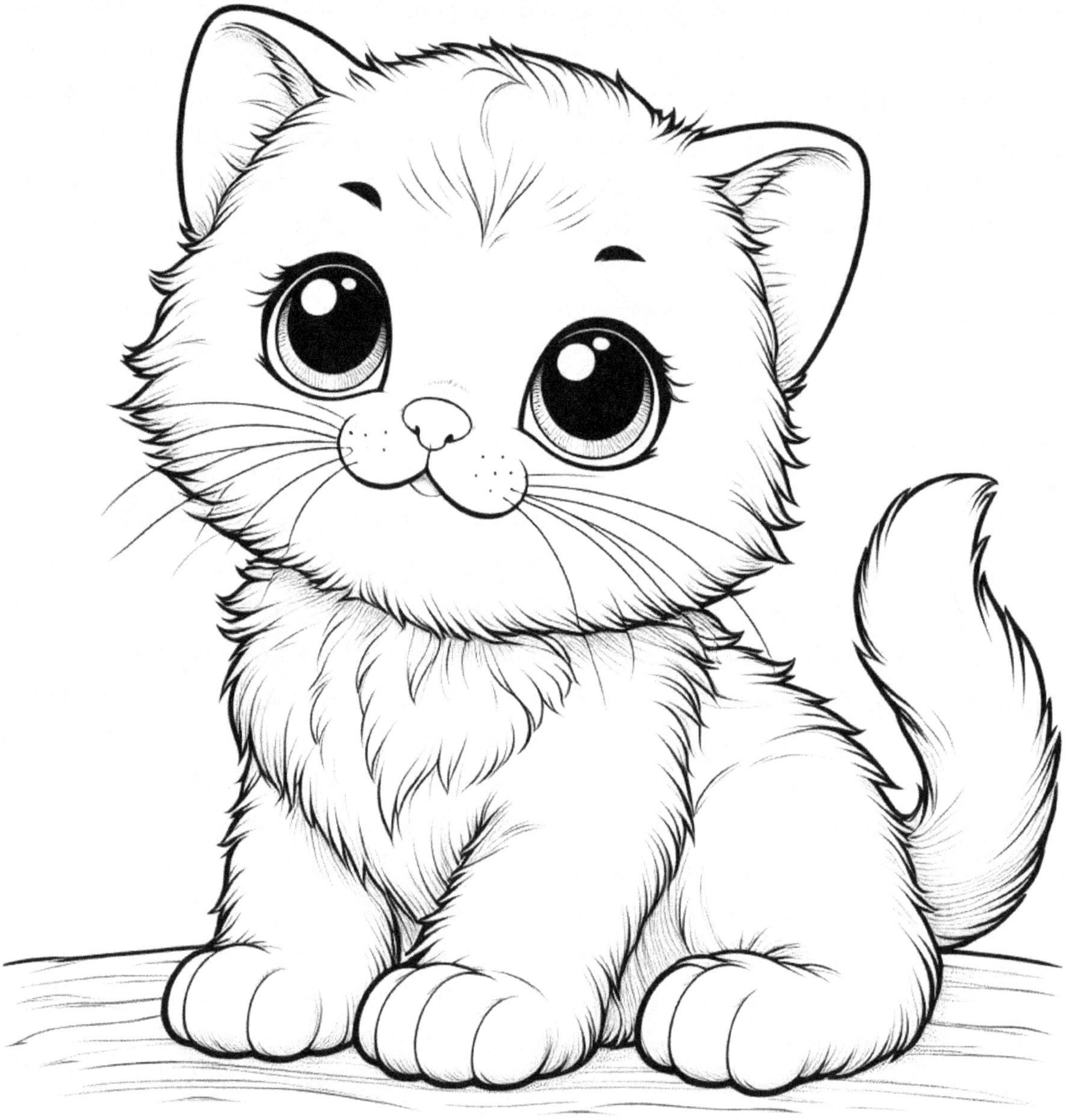

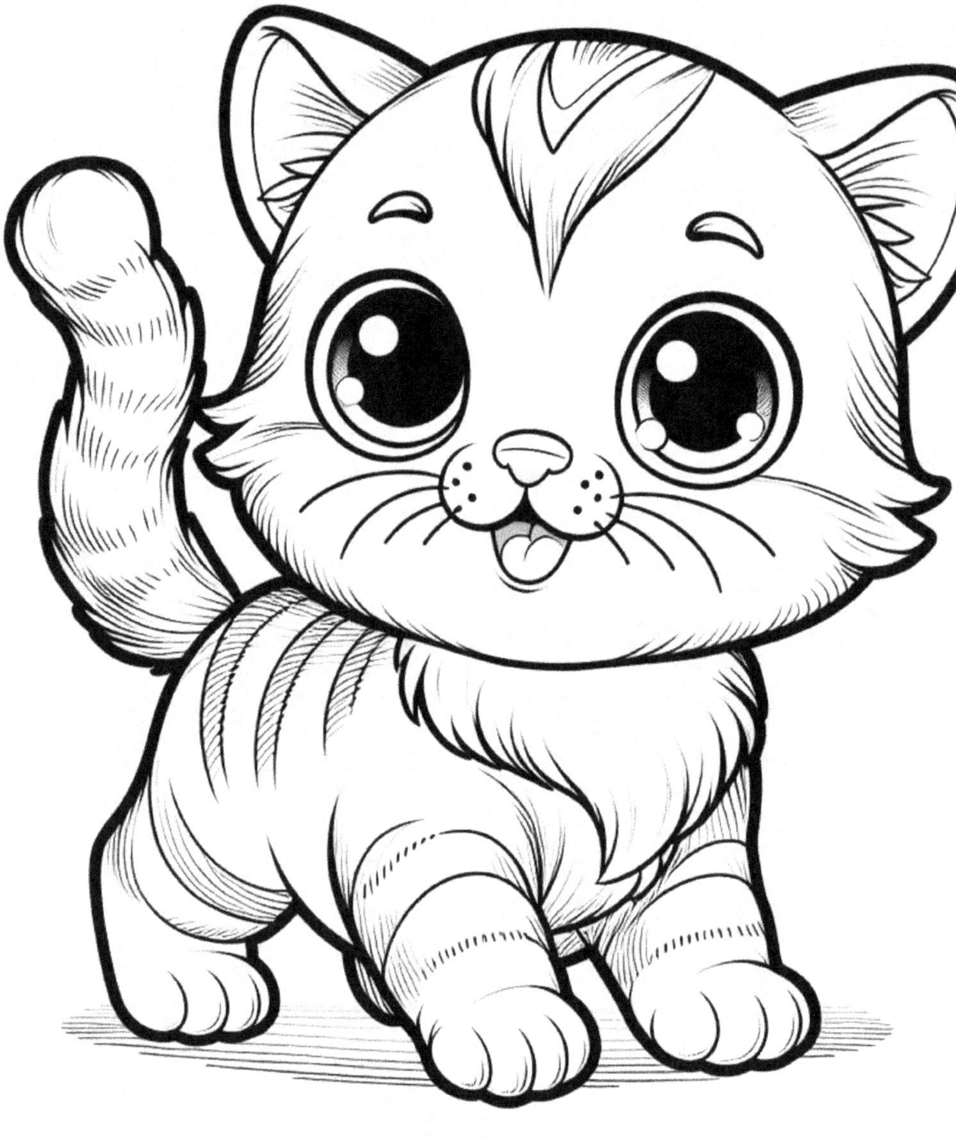

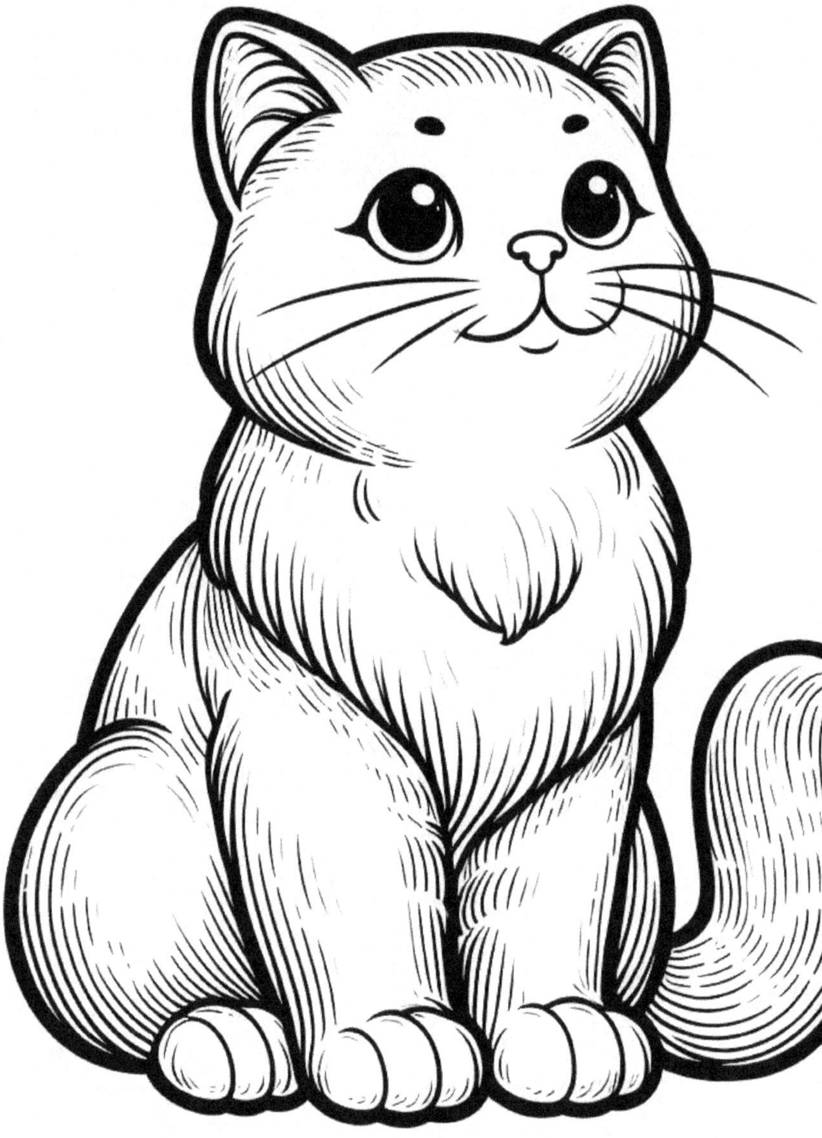

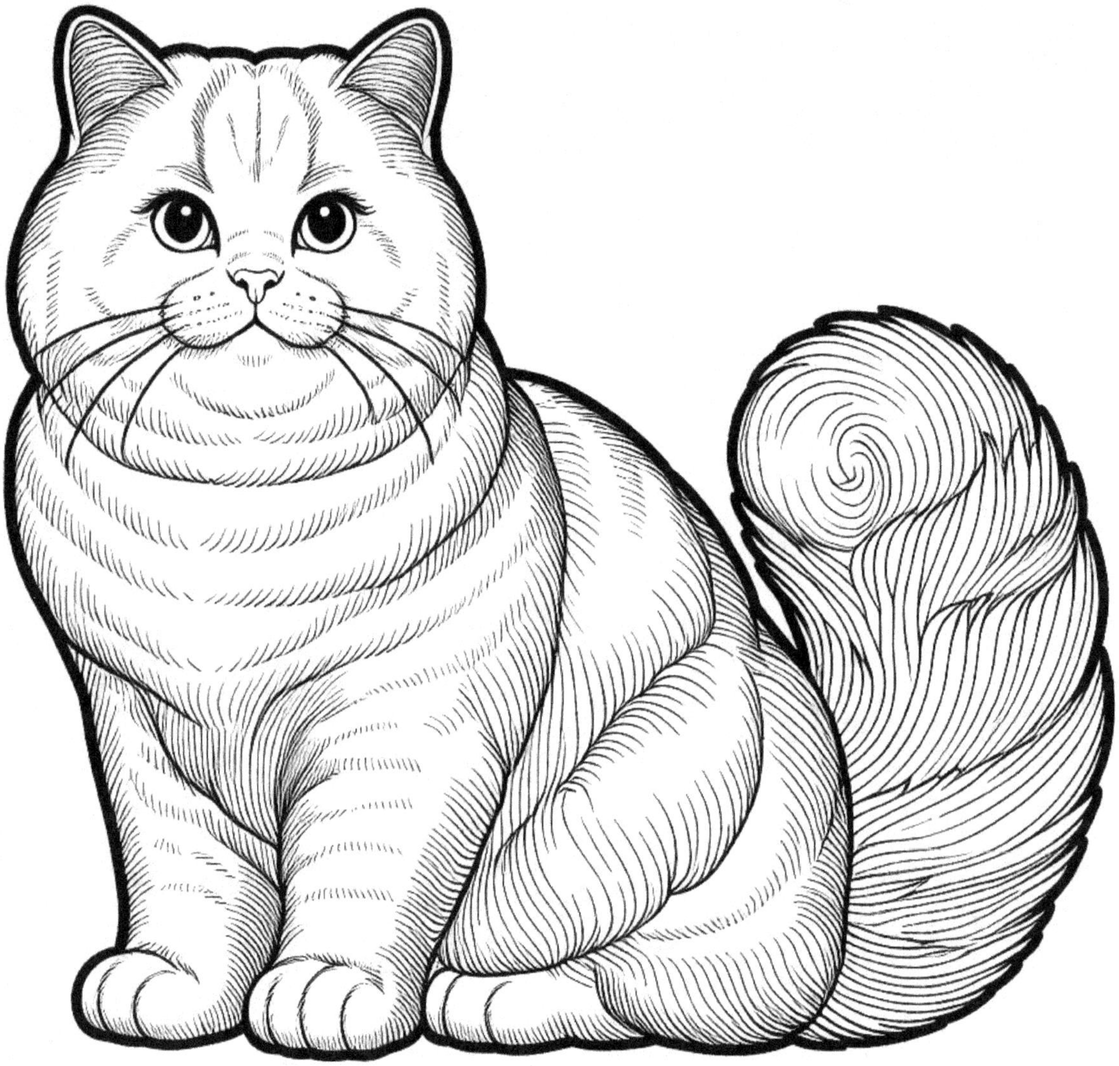

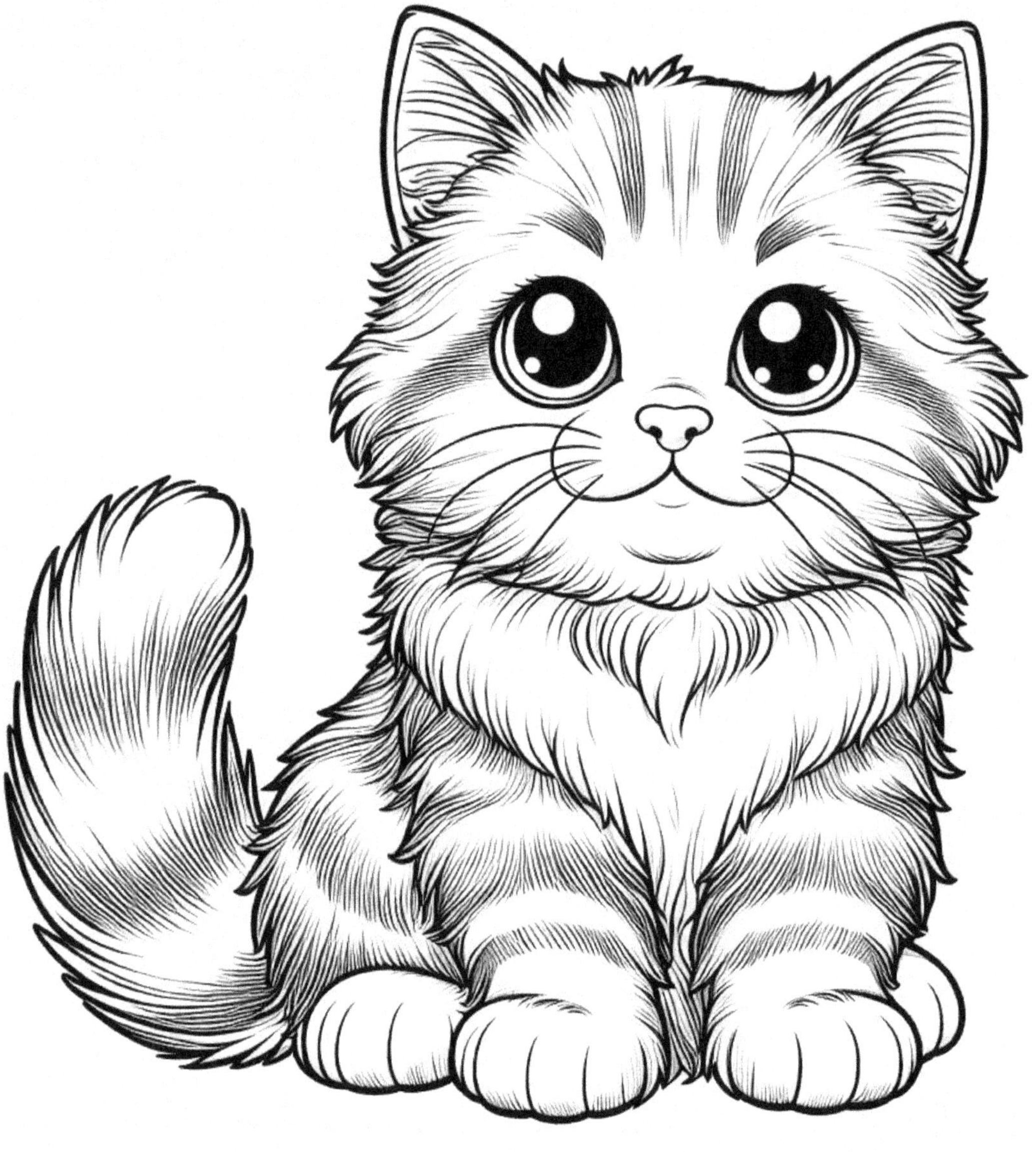

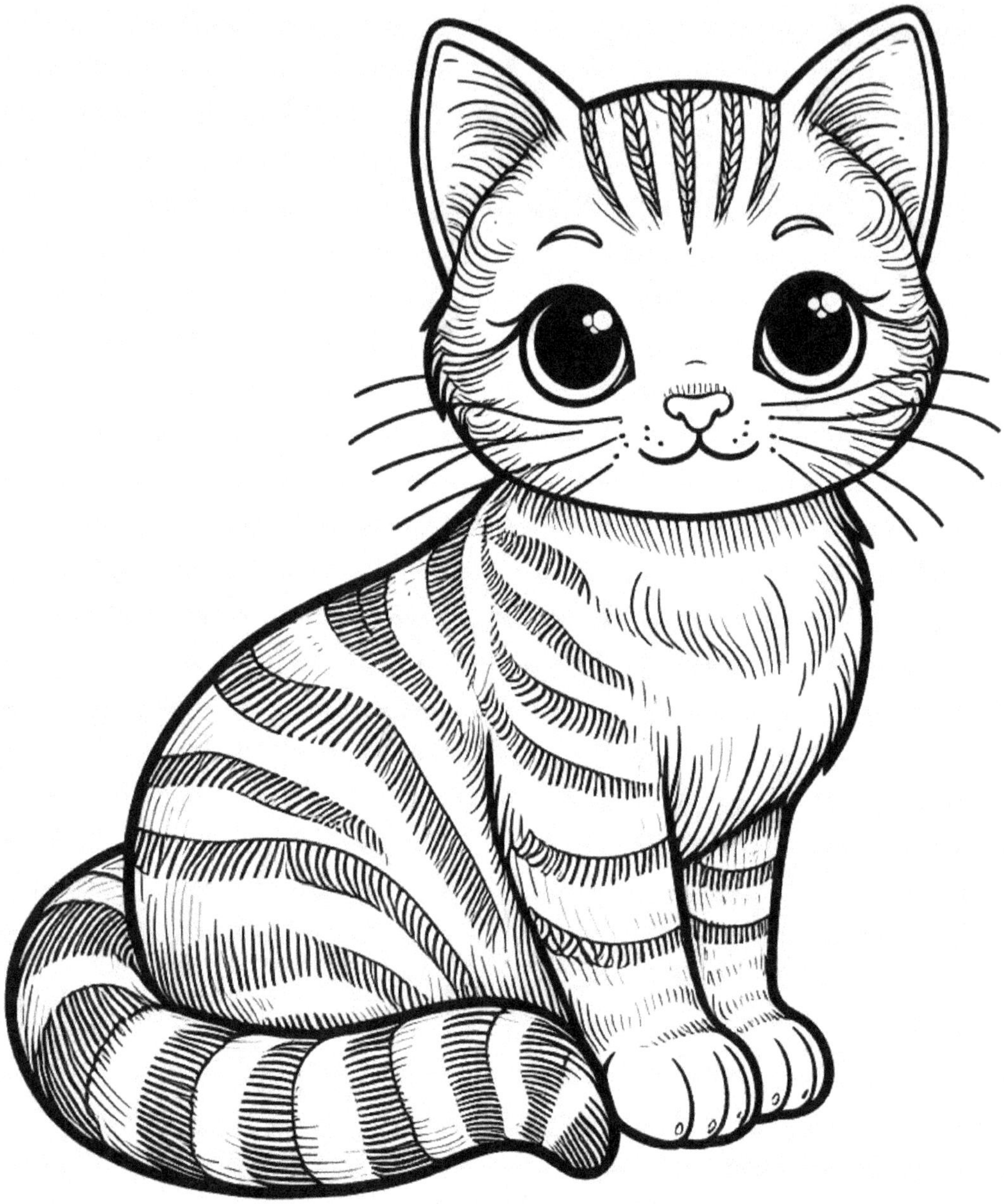

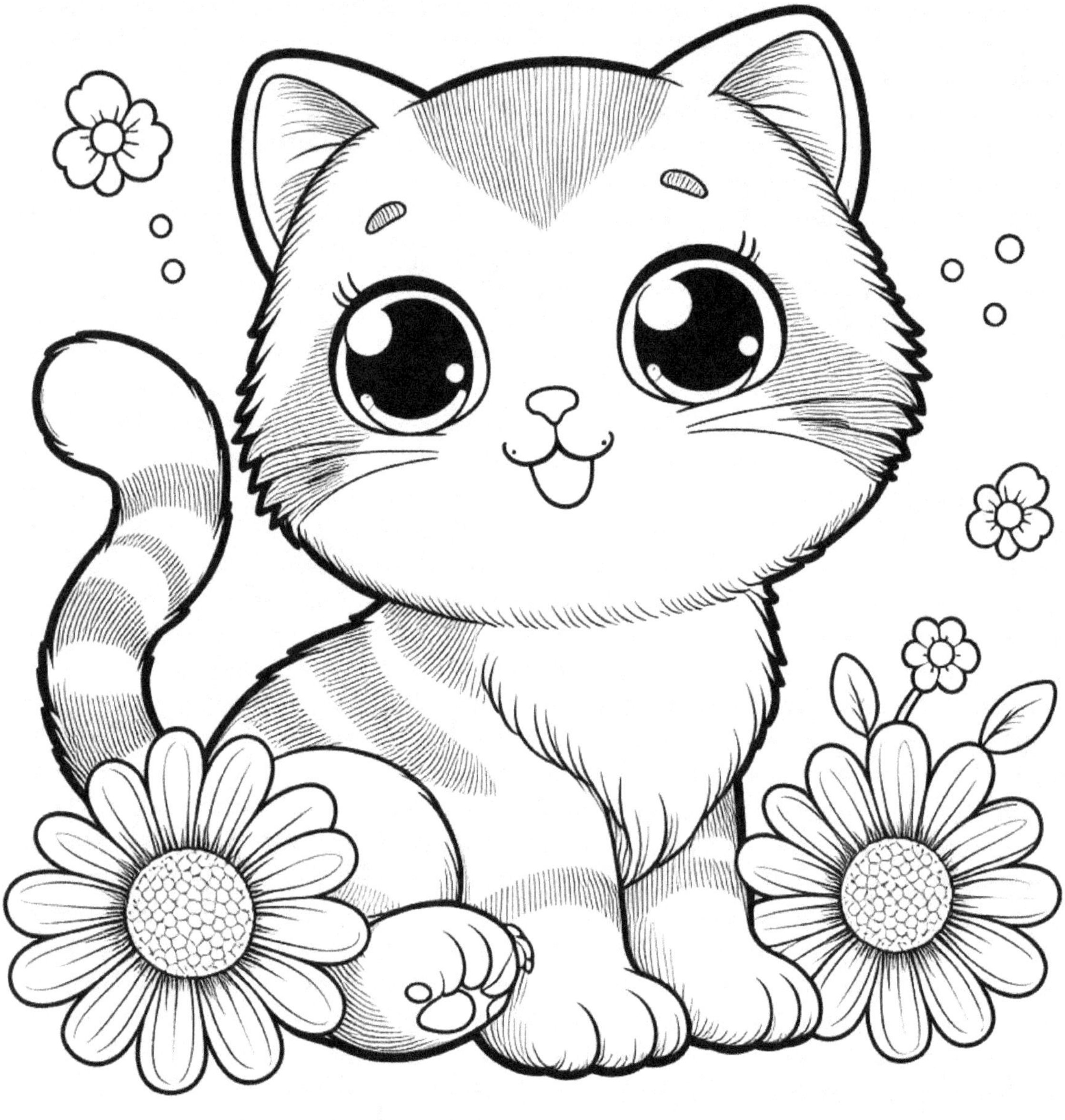

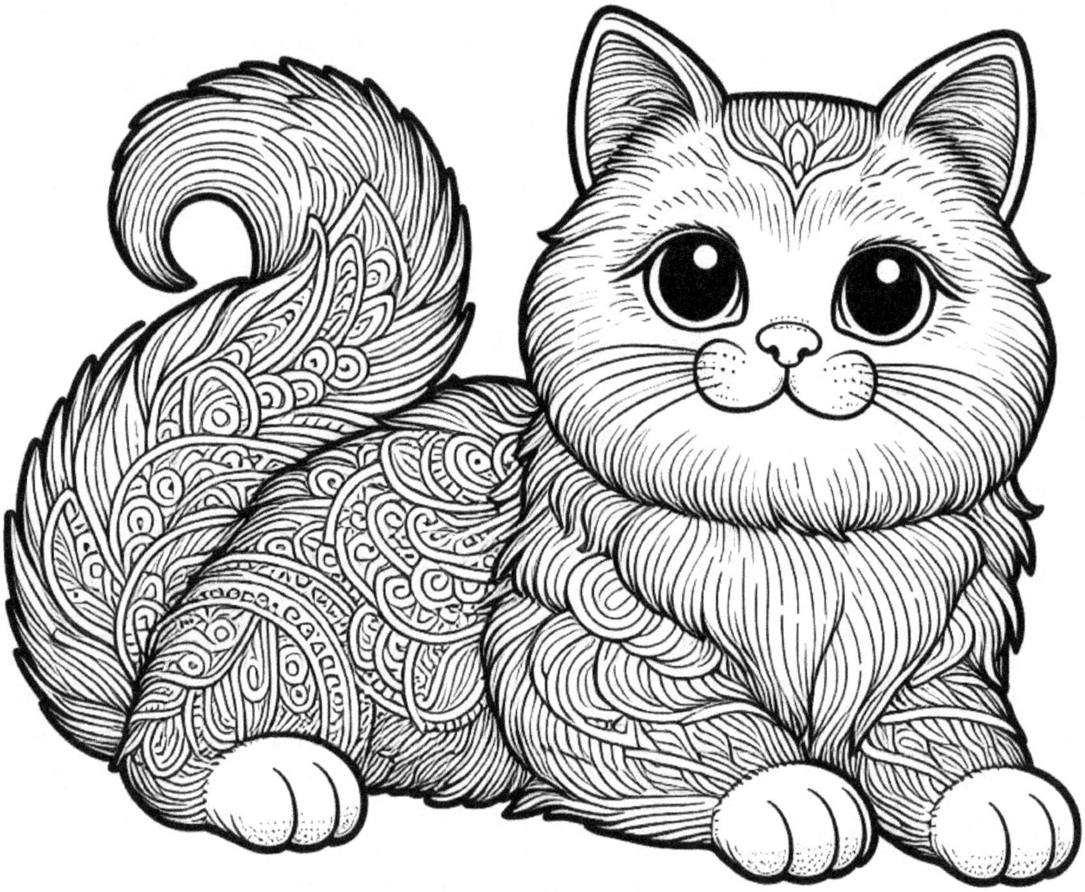

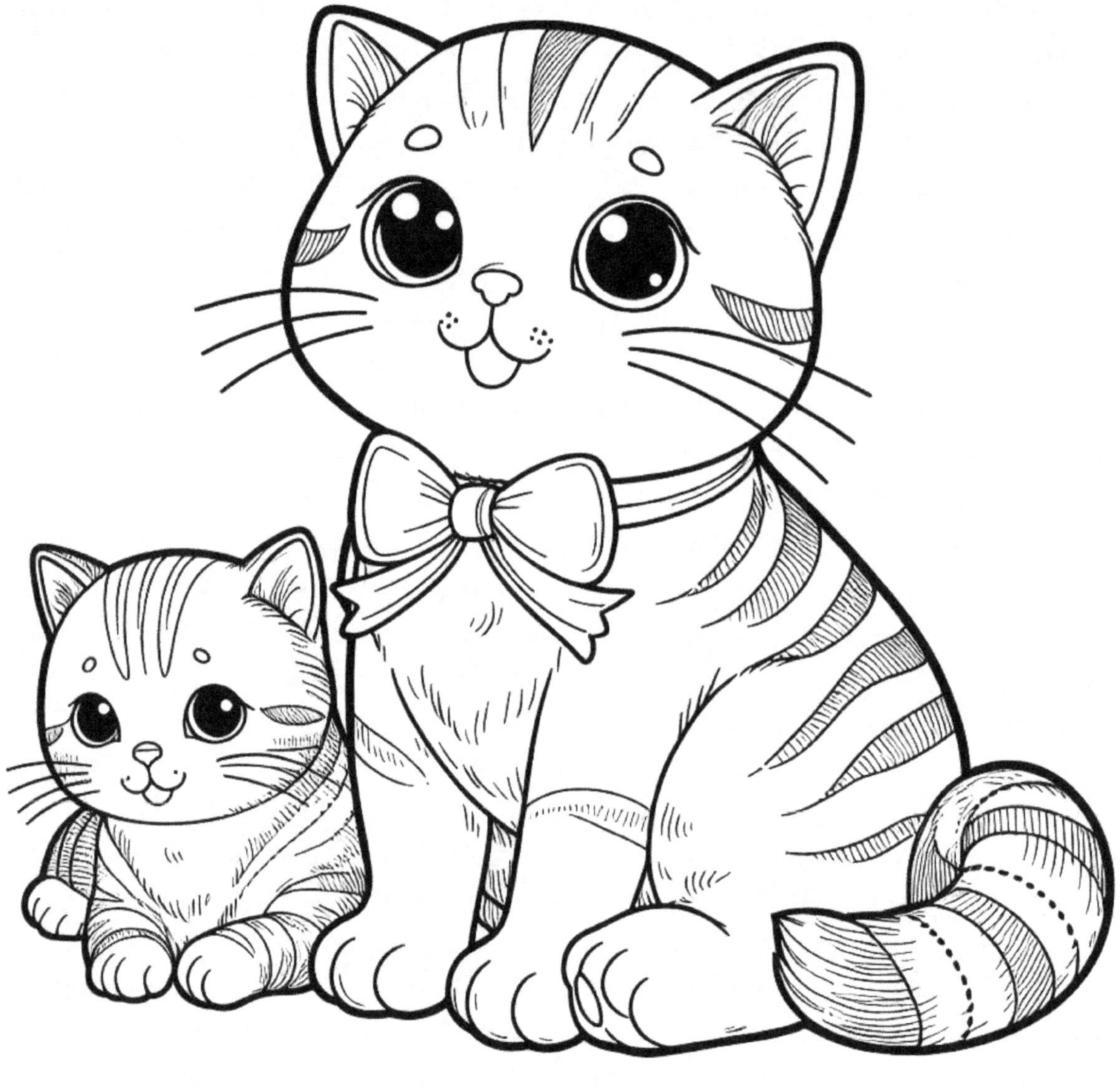

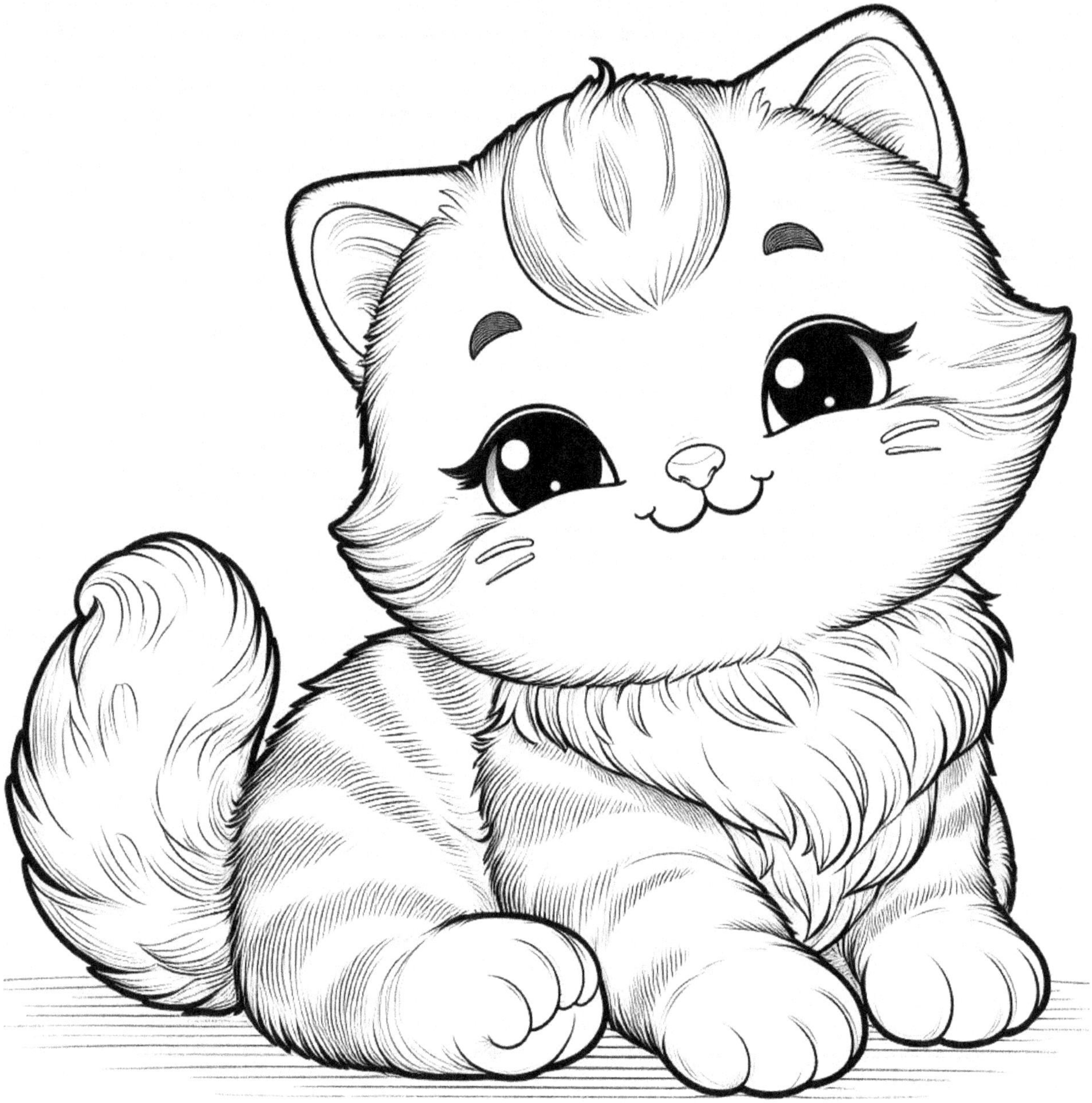

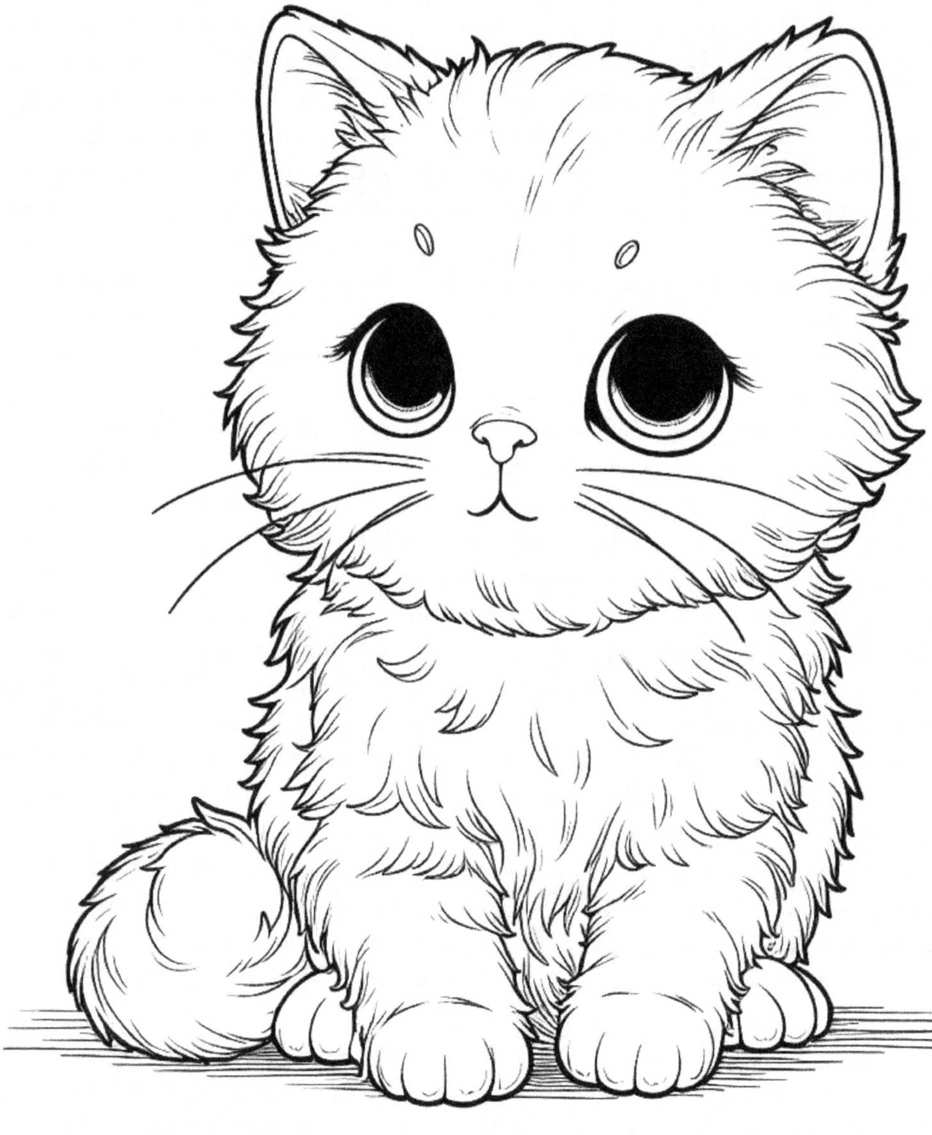

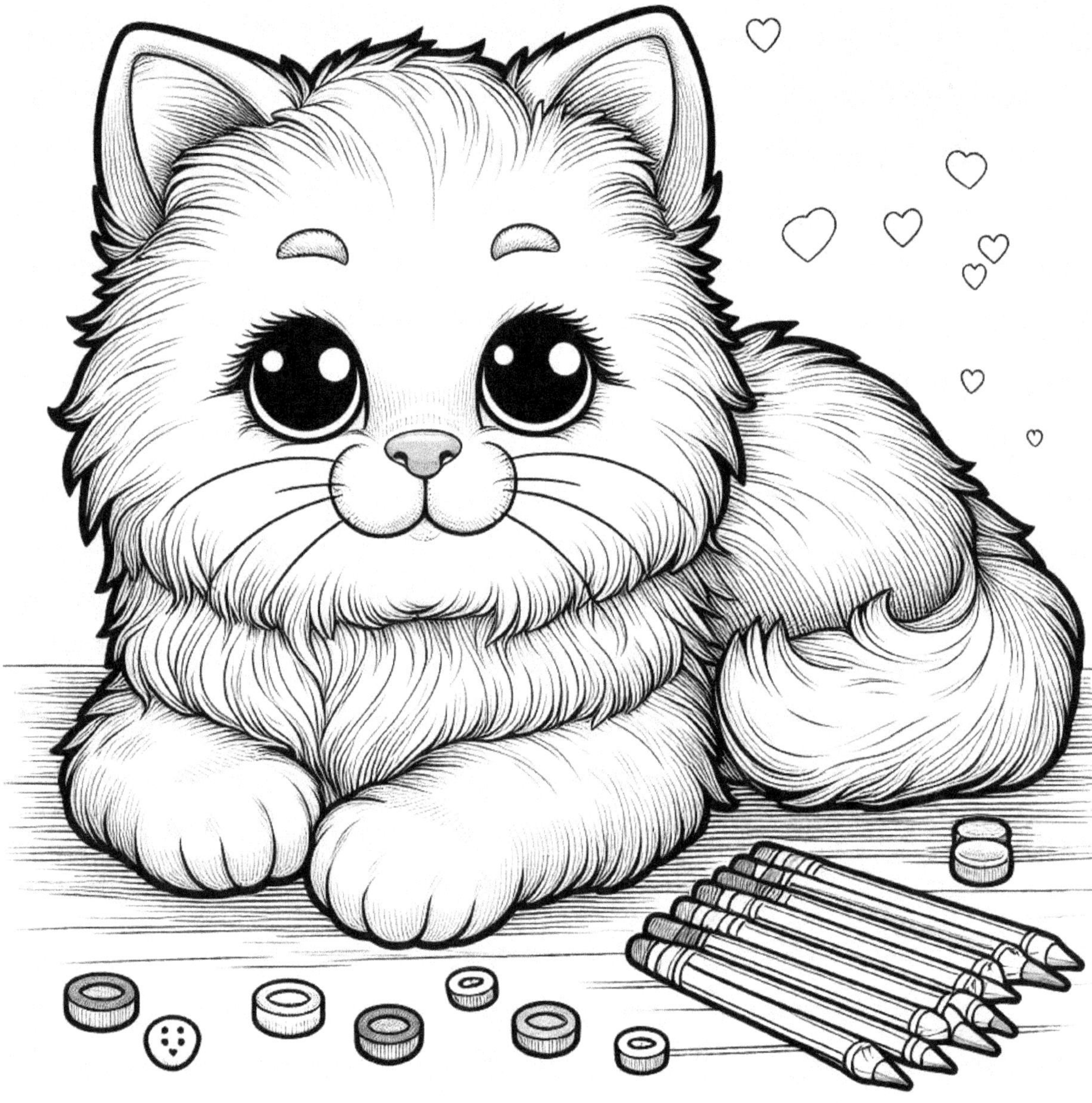

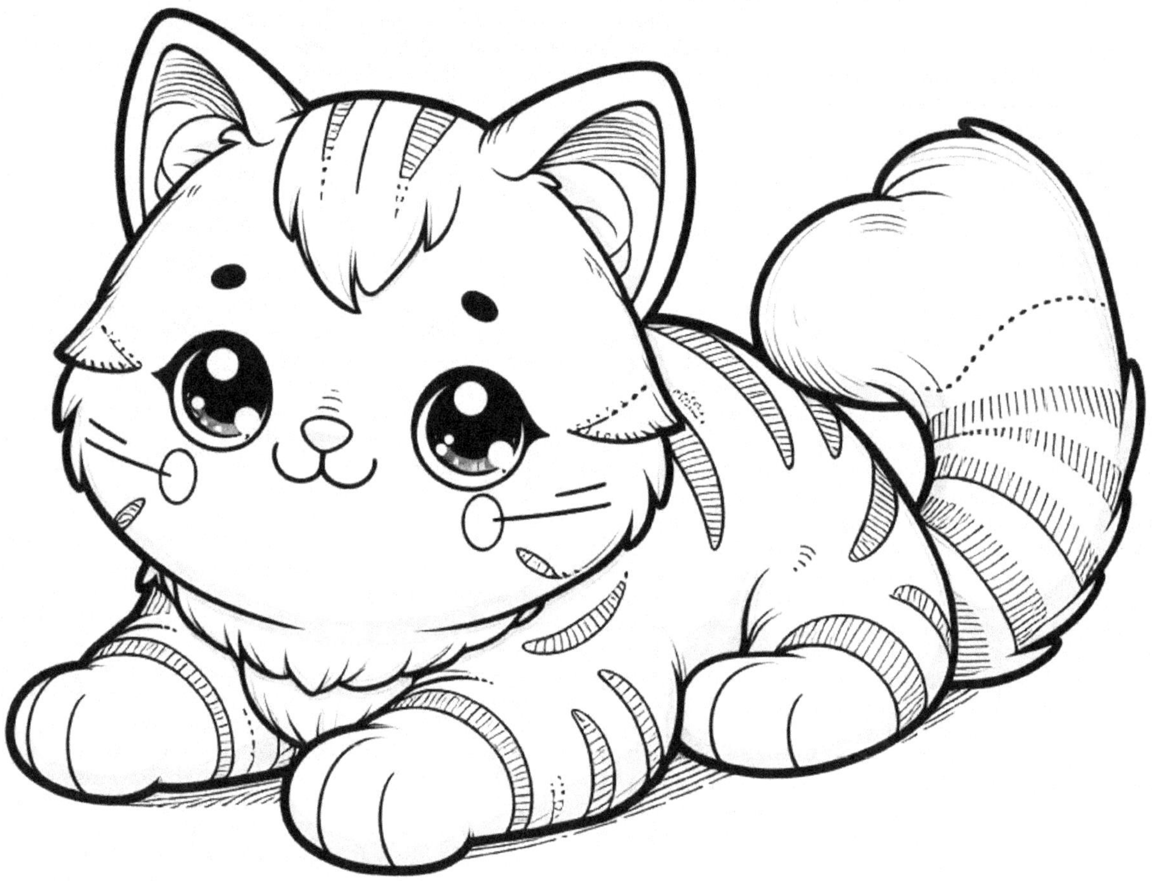

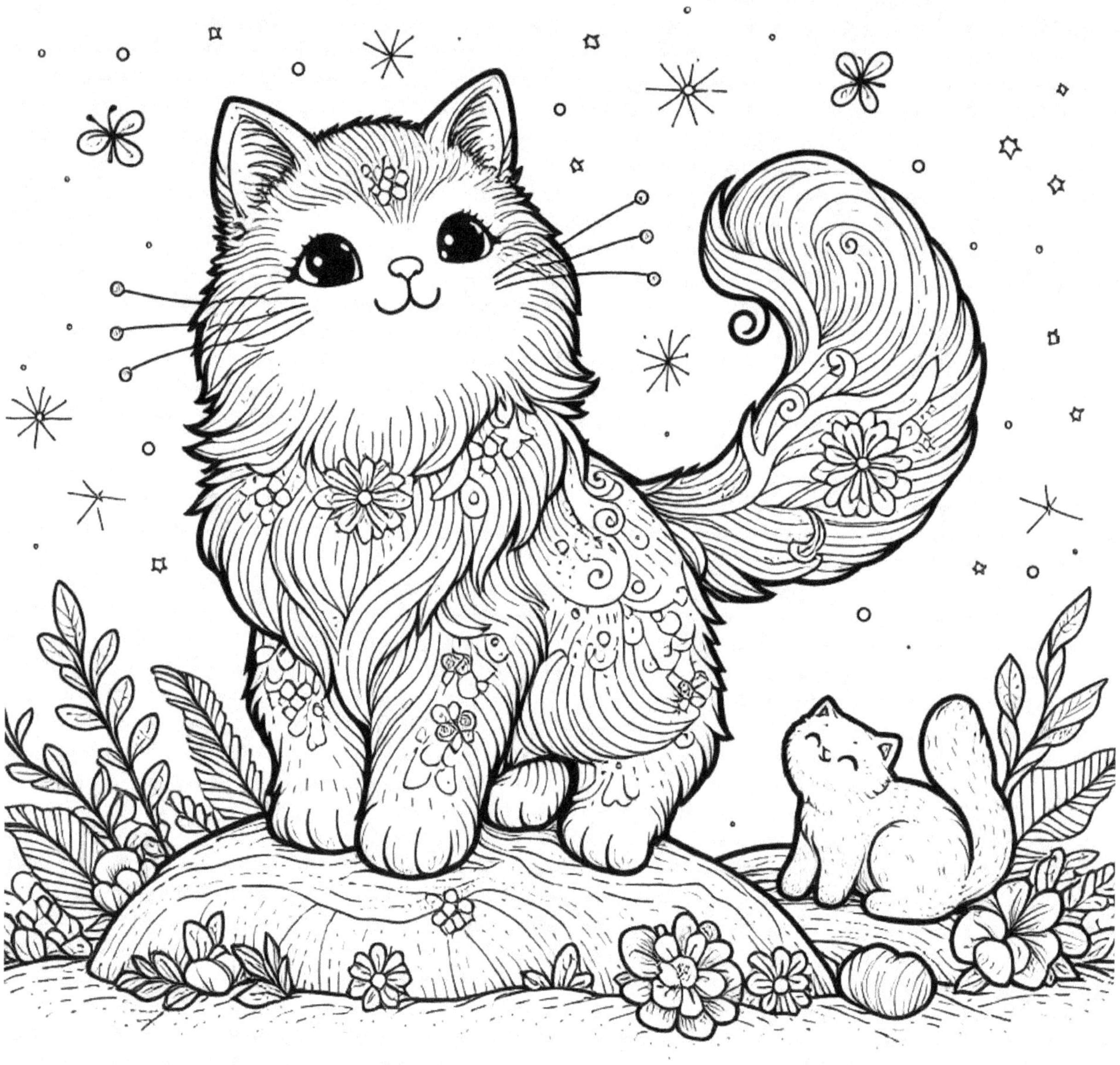

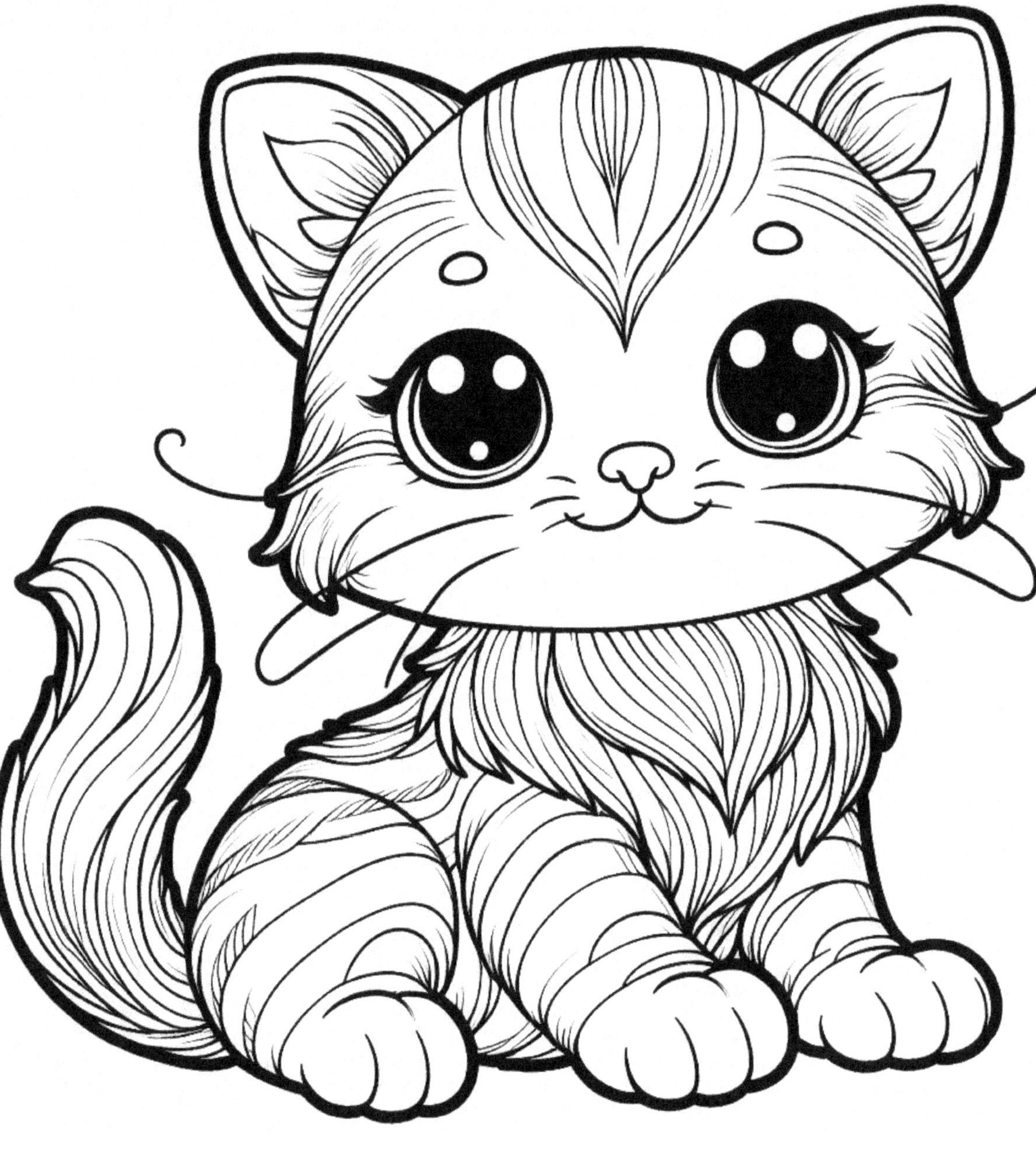

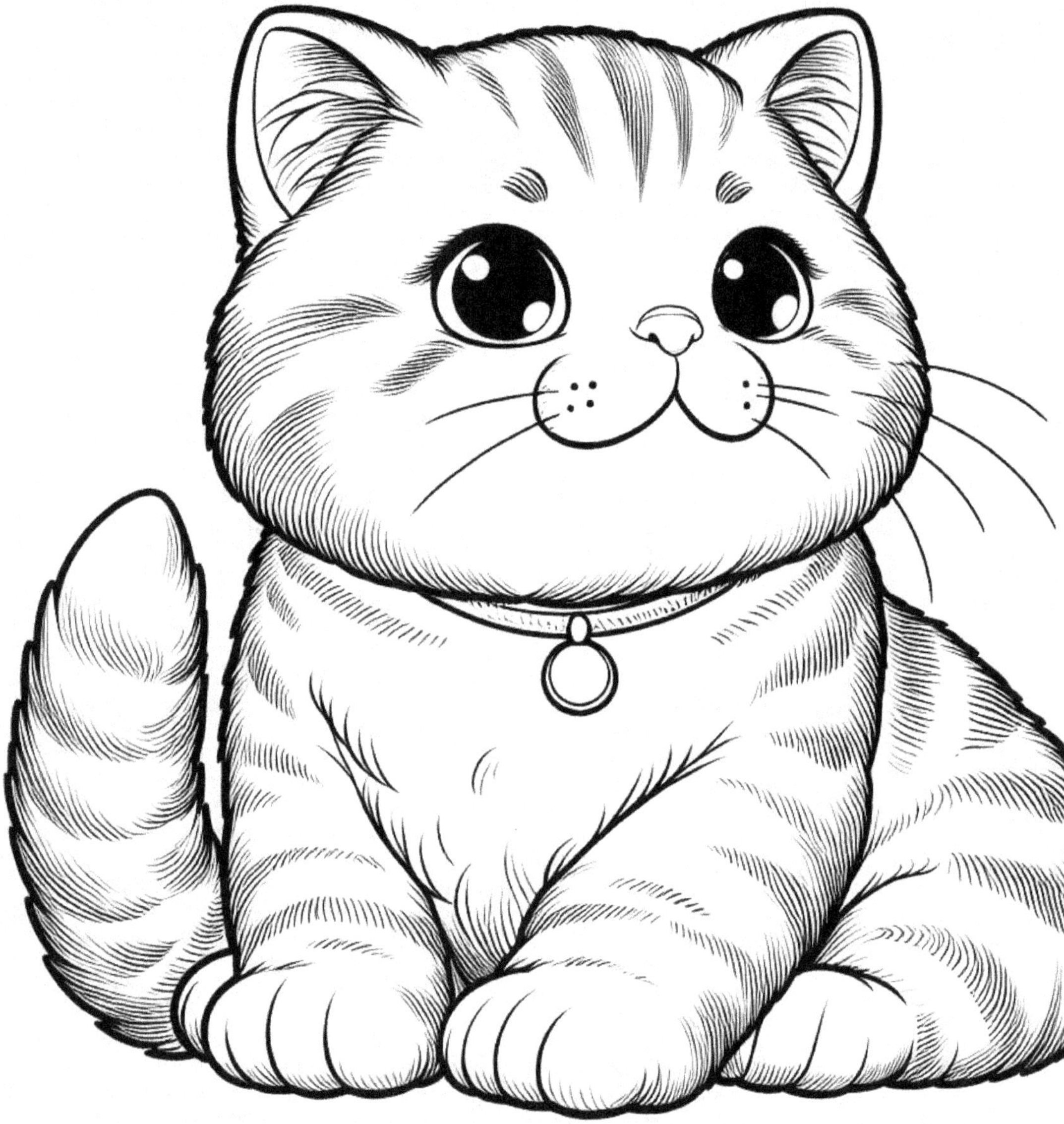

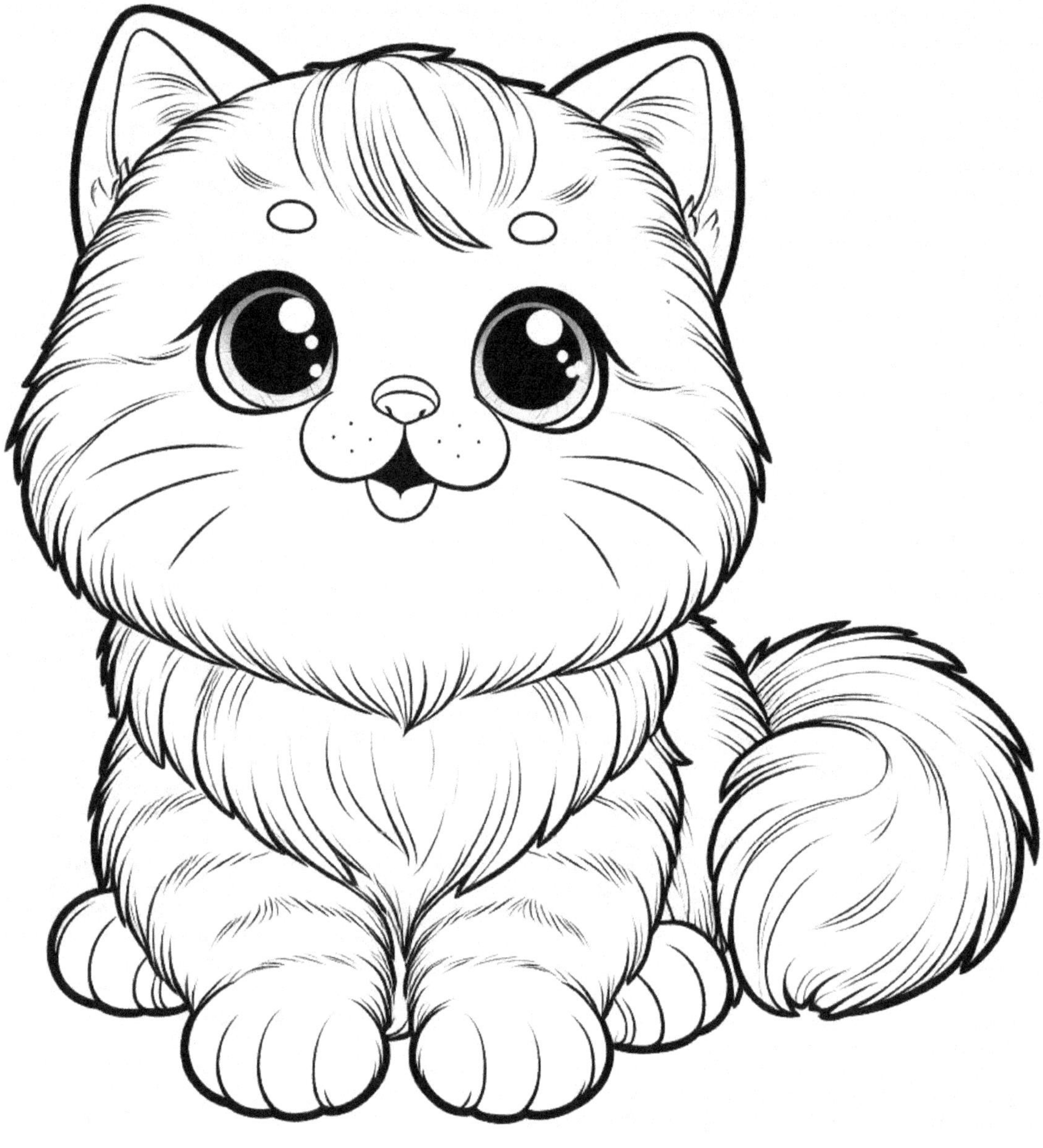

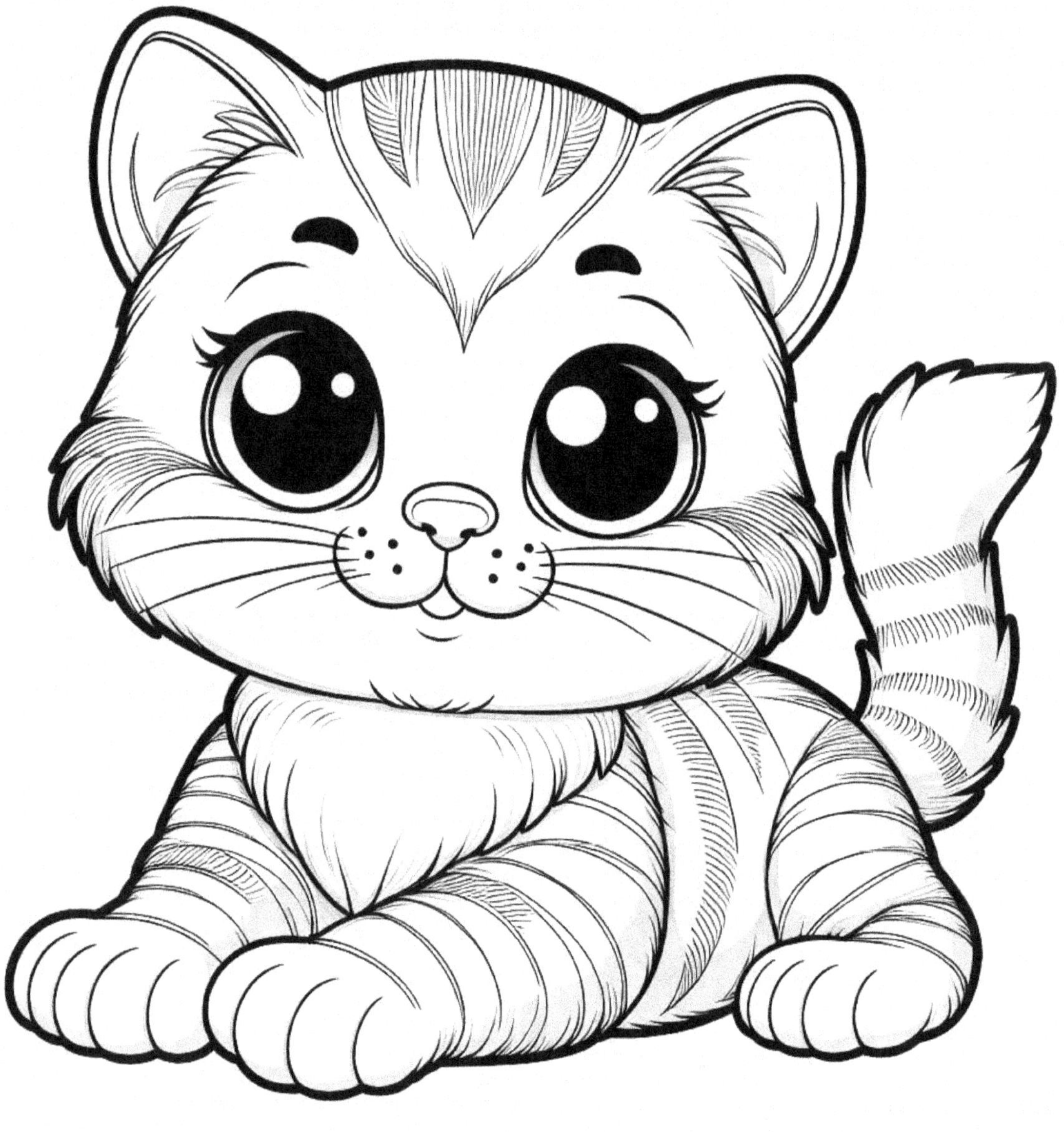

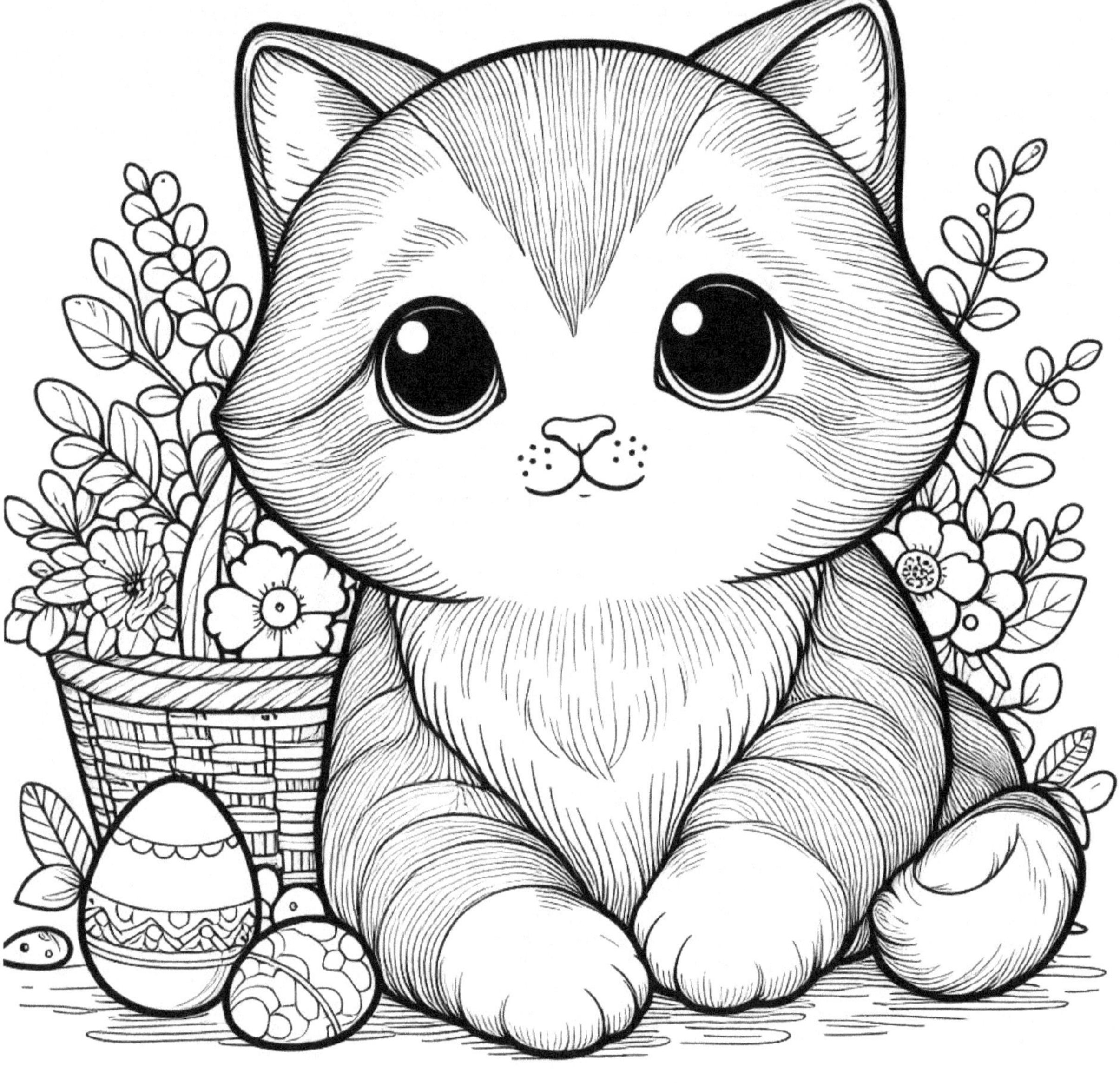

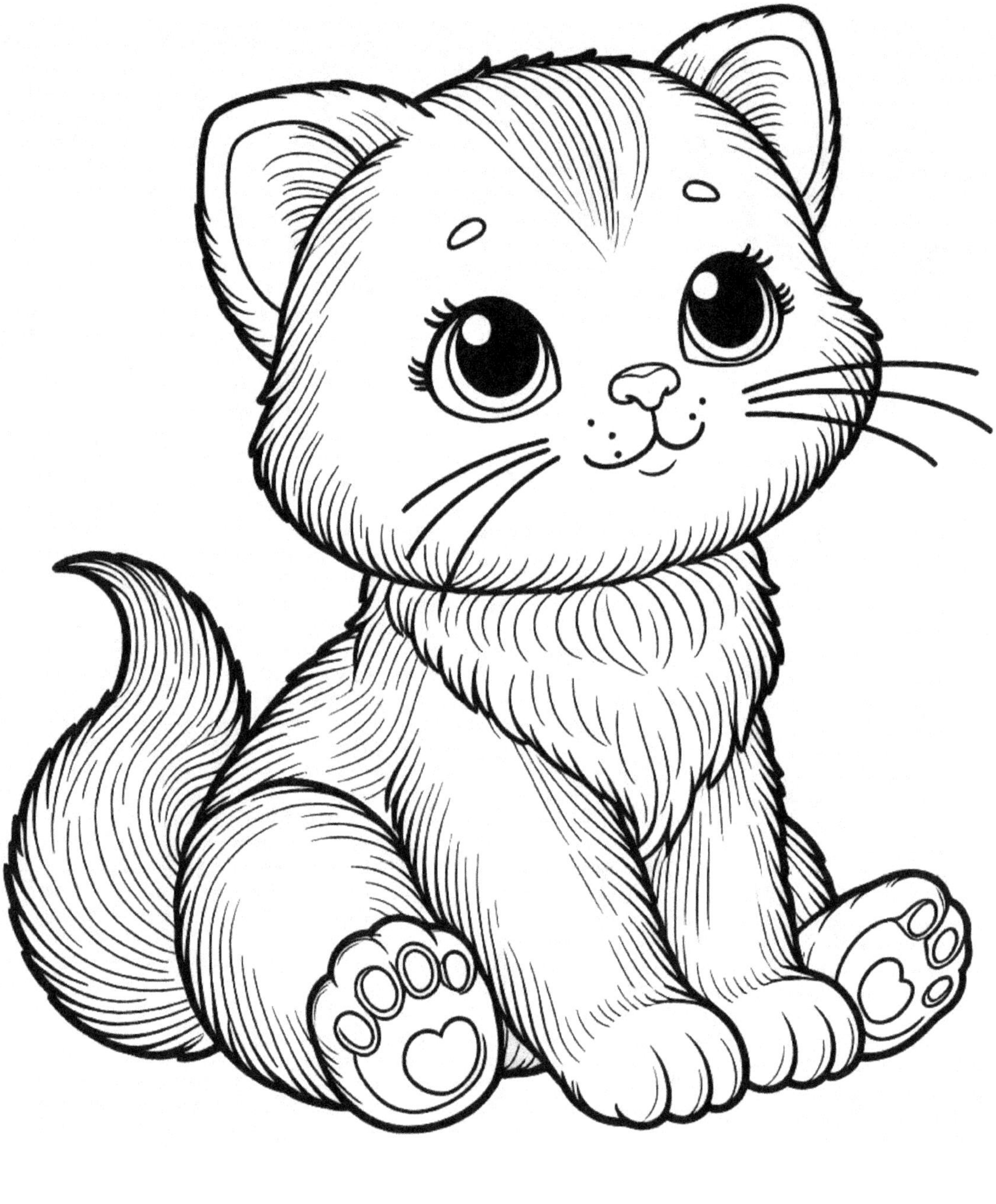

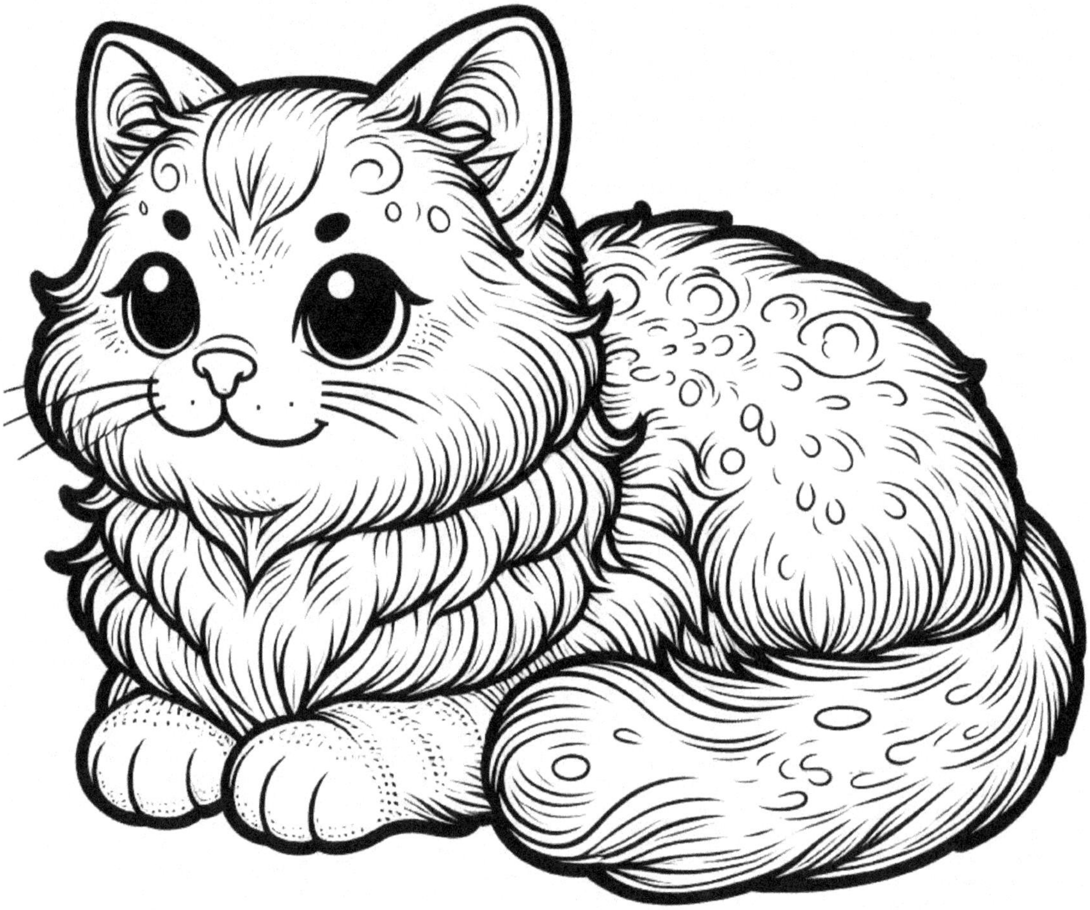

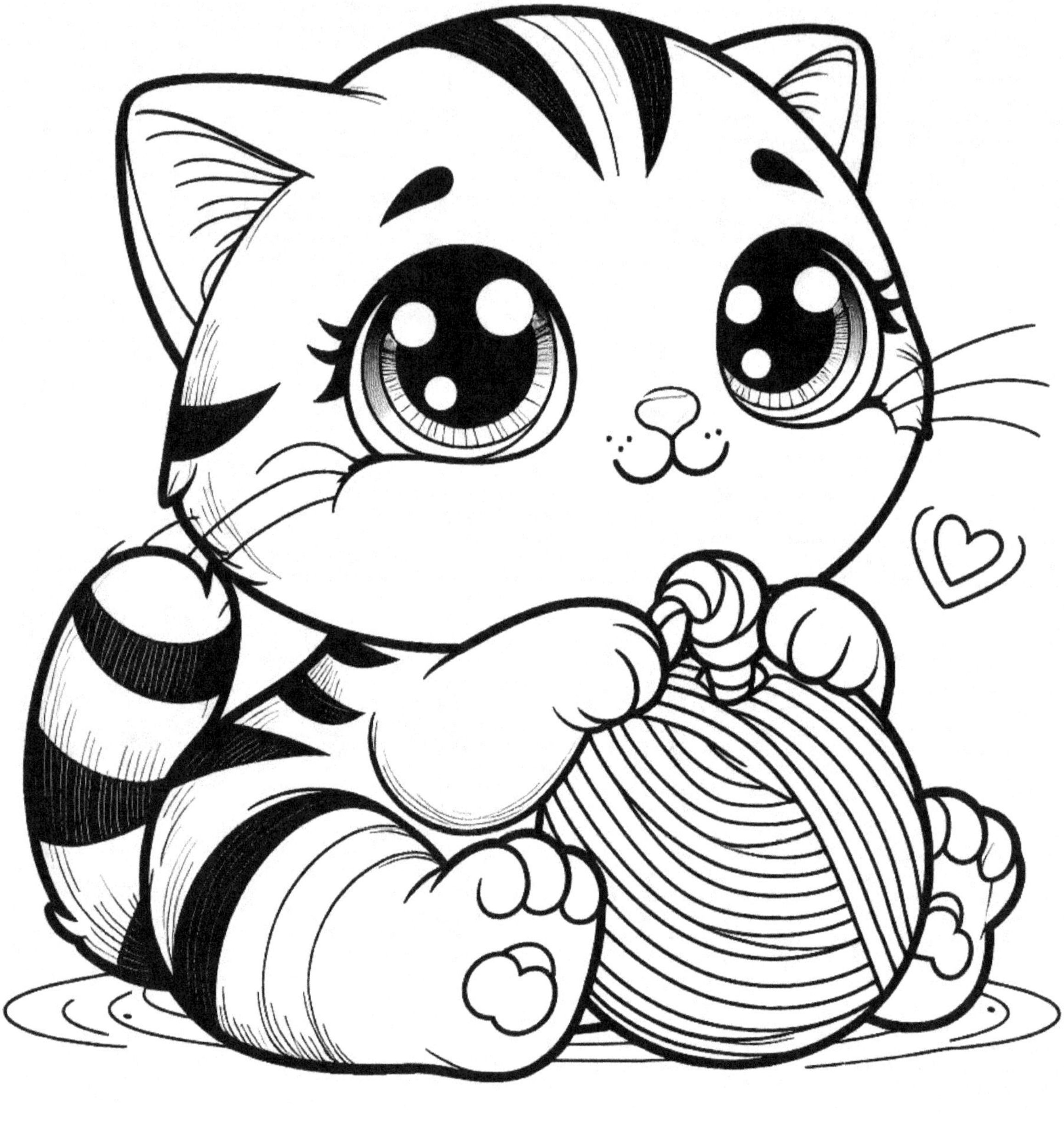

I Hope You
Enjoyed This
Coloring Book
XO

www.ingramcontent.com/pod-product-compliance
Lightning Source LLC
Chambersburg PA
CBHW060439220526
45465CB00008B/3200